LIGHTNING BOLT BOOKS™

Battlefront Military Machines

Brianna Kaiser

Lerner Publications ◆ Minneapolis

Copyright © 2025 by Lerner Publishing Group, Inc.

All rights reserved. International copyright secured. No part of this book may be reproduced, stored in a retrieval system, or transmitted in any form or by any means—electronic, mechanical, photocopying, recording, or otherwise—without the prior written permission of Lerner Publishing Group, Inc., except for the inclusion of brief quotations in an acknowledged review.

Lerner Publications Company
An imprint of Lerner Publishing Group, Inc.
241 First Avenue North
Minneapolis, MN 55401 USA

For reading levels and more information, look up this title at www.lernerbooks.com.

Main body text set in Billy Infant Regular. Typeface provided by SparkType.

Editor: Nicole Berglund **Photo Editor:** Nicole Berglund

Library of Congress Cataloging-in-Publication Data

Names: Kaiser, Brianna, 1996- author.
Title: Battlefront military machines / Brianna Kaiser.
Description: Minneapolis : Lerner Publications, [2025] | Series: Lightning bolt books : Mighty military vehicles | Includes bibliographical references and index. | Audience: Ages 6-9 | Audience: Grades 2-3 | Summary: "How do militaries fight enemies in combat? They use battlefront military machines. Readers will enjoy exploring the different parts of these machines and learning how they work to help soldiers complete missions"— Provided by publisher.
Identifiers: LCCN 2023038292 (print) | LCCN 2023038293 (ebook) | ISBN 9798765626153 (lib. bdg.) | ISBN 9798765628942 (pbk.) | ISBN 9798765635087 (epub)
Subjects: LCSH: Armored vehicles, Military—Juvenile literature. | Transportation, Military—Juvenile literature.
Classification: LCC UG446.5 .K175 2025 (print) | LCC UG446.5 (ebook) | DDC 623.74/75—dc23/eng/20230921

LC record available at https://lccn.loc.gov/2023038292
LC ebook record available at https://lccn.loc.gov/2023038293

Manufactured in the United States of America
1-1009907-51949-10/26/2023

Table of Contents

On a Mission — 4

So Many Sizes — 10

Transport — 16

Vehicle Diagram — 20

Fun Facts — 21

Glossary — 22

Learn More — 23

Index — 24

On a Mission

A large truck speeds across an open and bumpy field. It has to be quick! It is bringing soldiers to battle.

Another truck tows a broken vehicle away from the battle. Both trucks are battlefront military machines.

The broken vehicle can be fixed and used again.

Militaries use machines such as this Humvee in combat.

Militaries use these machines to help with missions. One type of mission is to deliver supplies to soldiers in battle.

Soldiers drive the machines. They sit in the cab. It is at the front of the vehicle.

Soldiers use a steering wheel to control the machines.

The machines have strong engines. Some of the machines have weapons.

A soldier controls a machine gun on top of the cab.

The machines are covered in armor. This special layer protects the soldiers inside from enemies.

So Many Sizes

Battlefront military machines come in different sizes. They can be light, medium, or heavy.

Light machines are smaller. Their size makes it easier for them to move and hide. **They can carry about four people.**

This machine carries a smaller machine inside.

Even though they are small, light machines can hold up to 500 pounds (227 kg) of supplies. That is about the weight of an adult grizzly bear!

Medium machines can do much more than light ones. They can hold up to 30,000 pounds (13,608 kg). That is heavier than an African elephant!

Medium machines can tow as much weight as they can hold!

Some medium machines have a cab roof that can fold down. That makes the machines shorter. Then they can fit into smaller spaces and hide better.

The cab

A crane

Some machines can have a winch. Winches can move other vehicles. Cranes can be used to lift things.

Transport

Militaries often use battlefront military machines for transport. Transport is moving things or people from one place to another.

Supplies can be stored inside the machines.

Soldiers may need food, water, and weapons. **The machines can transport supplies to soldiers.**

Battlefront machines get people where they need to go.

The machines can also move people or other vehicles. They may bring people or vehicles to and from a battle.

Militaries will keep working to make battlefront machines better. Watch for new machines in the future!

Vehicle Diagram

Humvee

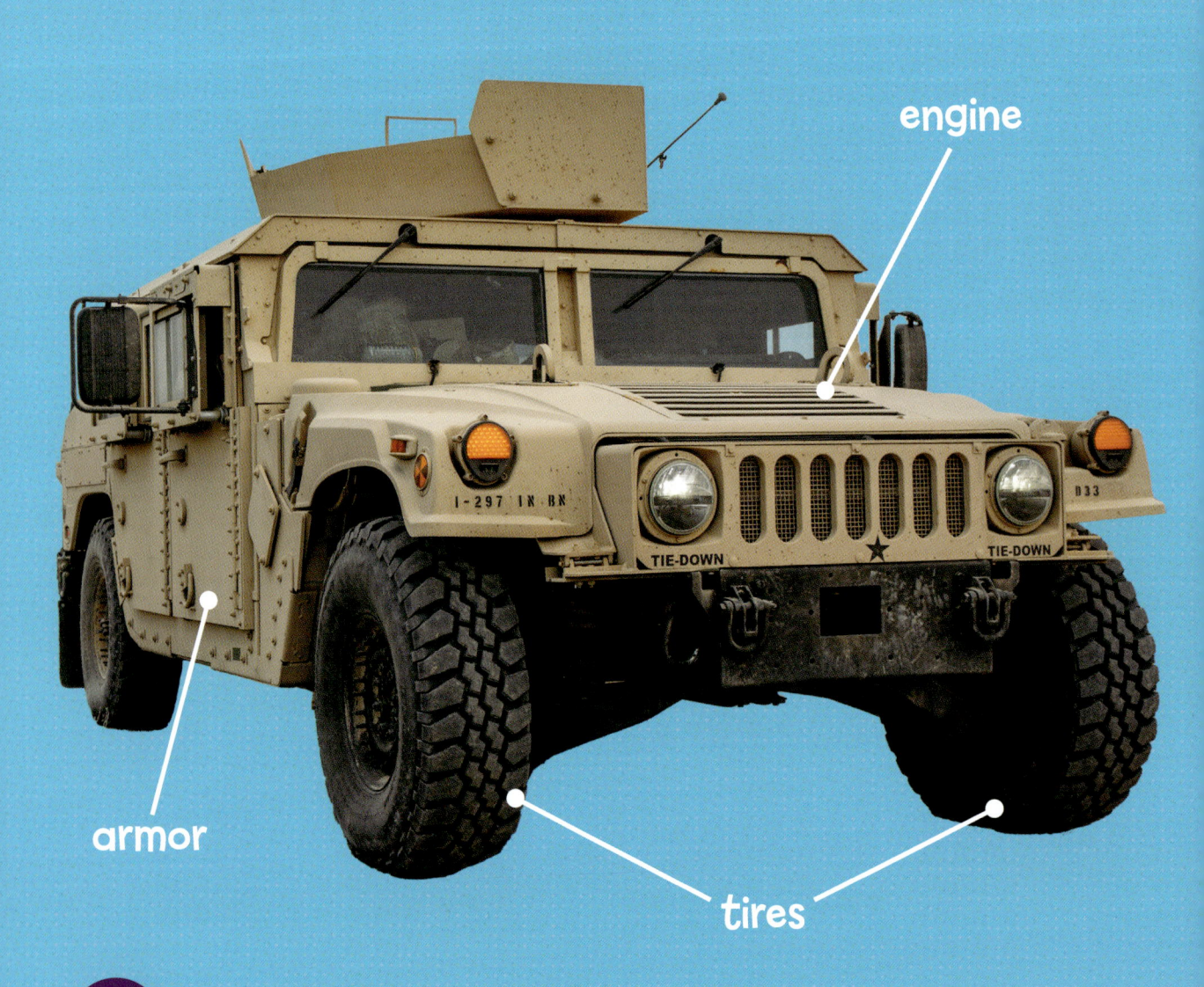

- engine
- armor
- tires

Fun Facts

- Winches and cranes can also be used for building things.

- Some battlefront military machines have tires that keep working even if they get a hole.

- Light and medium machines can be carried by some military planes and helicopters.

Glossary

armor: a special layer that covers machines to protect soldiers inside

battle: a fight

crane: a vehicle that lifts things

mission: an important task or goal a person or group works toward

supply: a tool for soldiers such as food, water, and weapons

transport: moving things or people from one place to another

winch: part of a vehicle that lifts other vehicles

Learn More

Britannica Kids: Army
https://kids.britannica.com/kids/article/army/352785

Ducksters: United States Armed Forces
https://www.ducksters.com/history/us_government/united_states_armed_forces.php

Hustad, Douglas. *US Army Equipment and Vehicles*. Minneapolis: Kids Core, 2022.

Kiddle: Ground Combat Vehicle Facts for Kids
https://kids.kiddle.co/Ground_Combat_Vehicle

Miller, Marie-Therese. *Land and Water Combat Vehicles*. Minneapolis: Lerner Publications, 2025.

Ringstad, Arnold. *The Military Vehicles Encyclopedia*. Minneapolis: Abdo Reference, 2024.

Index

armor, 9

engine, 8

mission, 6

soldier, 4, 6-7, 9, 17

transport, 16-17

truck, 4-5

Photo Acknowledgments

Image credits: U.S. Army National Guard photo by Pvt. Joseph Burns, pp. 4, 6, 20; U.S. Marine Corps photo by Staff Sgt. David L. Proffitt, p. 5; Photo by Capt. Andy Thaggard, 155th Armored Brigade Combat Team, p. 7; U.S. Army Reserve photo by Master Sgt. Michel Sauret, p. 8; U.S. Army photo by Spc. Jonathan Wallace, p. 9; U.S. Army photo by Staff Sgt. Justin A. Moeller, 40th Public Affairs Detachment, p. 10; U.S. Marine Corps photo by Sgt. Manuel A. Serrano, pp. 11, 12; Photo by Sgt. 1st Class Phillip Eugene, 80th Training Command, p. 13; Pretendo at English Wikipedia/Wikimedia Commons (CC), p. 14; Wikimedia Commons (PD), p. 15; Sgt. Demetrius Munnerlyn/Wikimedia Commons (PD), p. 16; Photo by Staff Sgt. John Couffer, 1st Armored Brigade Combat Team, 1st Cavalry Division, p. 17; U.S. Army photo by Scott T. Sturkol, Public Affairs Office, Fort McCoy, Wis., p. 18; Photo by Nadine Wiley De Moura, 688th Cyberspace Wing, p. 19.

Cover: U.S. Army photo by Georgios Moumoulidis.